IN MY THOUGHTS
THE EVOLUTION OF A
SCARRED MIND

IN MY THOUGHTS
THE EVOLUTION OF A SCARRED MIND
Copyright © 2024 Jerry Mason

Printed in the United States of America.

ISBN-13: 979-8-218-57229-7

Contact Information:
AuthorJerryMason@gmail.com

Cover & Interior Design by
Carlos V. Kaigler/ C'vaughn'K Graphic Designs/
Author The Poet B.GKL

IN MY THOUGHTS
THE EVOLUTION OF A
SCARRED MIND

Author Jerry *"Bobo"* Mason

Titles by Author Jerry "Bobo" Mason

COACH *"The Mediator of Dreams and Destroyer of Generations"*

I WAS ONLY FOUR-YEARS-OLD:
"The Psyche Of A Broken Sole"

Dedication

~To my family for all the love, support, communication, stability, and laughter.

~To our Dad for hanging tough and being there for us.

~To our beautiful Mom. May she rest in Peace. I hope that you are happy, healthy, and proud of us every day. I also need you to help me sell a lot of books. We Love and Miss you.

~To all the people struggling every day emotionally, mentally, and physically. Keep praying and pushing. You and your story matter.

Contents

Foreword

I remember Bobo telling us made-up stories using his imaginary character, Matthew.

Although Matthew was in Bobo's fictional mind, he was passionate, animated, and very believable in his storytelling.

He made Cedric and I feel Matthew was real and was a part of the present scene he created.

Ced, Bobo, and I shared a room. I had the top bunk bed, Bobo the bottom, and Ced a twin bed beside us. There was barely enough room in the room for anything else.

Bobo utilized the space in between the beds to sometimes stand up and create the vision he felt and wanted us to feel.

Through some of our roughest nights or times, we needed Bobo and Matthew. He always had a sense of what was needed at the time. Even though his temper sometimes got the best of him and the moment.

Once Bobo got mad about something and told Ced and I that Matthew wasn't real. That all the stories he'd told us were not real but made up.

We were pissed at him and felt betrayed and violated. More than anything, we were mad Matthew wasn't real. But that was just one of the many moods and personalities Bobo had.

I didn't know at the time Matthew was someone Bobo created in his head to help him deal with the lonely pain he was enduring and he felt only Matthew would listen to him.

I remember getting into fights with Bobo all the time. Mainly fights that involved me putting him into a headlock or using moves I learned from watching wrestling.

He was always agitating and instigating the altercations and I always won. But he would say differently.

Bobo was very competitive and hated to lose, at anything. When we would play cards for candy and when he would lose consecutive times, he would pick up the cards and throw them so no one else could play.

His temper most times got the best of him. He and I were born in the same year. I was born in January, and he was born in December. That meant for about two weeks, we were the same age. I hated it and he knew it.

So, he would provoke a fight because he knew he could get under my skin, and I would engage. As we grew older, we shared the same friends but hung out with different ones in our group. Also, since we were so close in age, we always played together in all sports.

I don't remember him and me talking about sports. We just both knew each other wanted to be the best and we both hated losing.
I lived with my grandmother for about two years during high school. Bobo was always somewhere doing only God knew what. We saw each other at school, practices, or places where we played sports.

We played together for two complete seasons on the varsity basketball team. We never discussed how we'd play or anything about our opponents.

That didn't matter to us. We knew if we came to play, which we ALWAYS did, along with our teammates, we would be very hard to beat.

Through that journey, building our own identity, stardom, and fan base, we inherited the name, *"The Mason Combination."*

Although we had very different personalities, we were tough together every time we stepped on the court. We all knew the pressures of being a Lamesa Golden Tornado basketball player and we all handled our responsibility to that tradition with care, respect, and greatness.

There would be times I'd come home late from partying with friends, a concert or just being out and Bobo would be in the street or yard jumping rope in a weighted vest. I always told people that was the difference between being recruited by a handful of colleges and being recruited by almost every university in the nation.

However, no matter what, me and my siblings were always about our business. Especially when it came to sports and our survival.

From the time Coach Roberts moved Bobo to the varsity team at the end of his freshman season, he was the best player I ever played with and against.

We only played together or on the same team during real games. While playing at the Boys & Girls Club, park, gym, or anywhere else, we played on opposite teams and always guarded each other.

Because we both HATED losing more than we liked winning, we'd battle for every rebound, loose ball, and made each earn every bucket we made. He made me better. I made him better.

Mine and his battles made everyone around us better. We all created a culture and standard that brought Lamesa basketball back to the prominence and dominance it once had.

Playing against and with Bobo prepared me for college basketball. Playing against and with Bobo assisted me in being inducted into my college's basketball Hall of Fame.

Playing with and against Bobo made him a first-team high school All-American, one of the best recruits in the nation, and a Division I athlete.

As we have grown older, we talked more about our respect for one another's greatness with others than we did amongst ourselves.

I feel the respect we have for each other for the things we achieved as "The Mason Combination" and individually is way more than words can express.

It's just known between us. Whenever we are in public together, our presence is still omnipotent when people we played against see us or someone who watched us play together.

They still remember and will never forget the impact we left on high school basketball in the state of Texas.
Bobo was a different breed with his character and personality.

The fact that he competed the way he did, at the level that he did, and achieved all he achieved with the horrible injuries he was dealing with, fascinates me to this day.

Injuries that he kept from everyone for reasons only he can explain. It's mind-blowing.

I can only imagine how his injuries affected him physically, emotionally, and socially.

It makes me sad as a brother and at the same time very proud to love and call him my brother.

I'm very excited and interested to read his 3rd Novel, IN *MY THOUGHTS "THE EVOLUTION OF A SCARRED MIND."*
The depth of his material encompasses so many realistic situations we all struggle with and deal with daily.

His willingness to share his trauma and relay that through the quotes that have gotten him through some of his darkest moments makes this a must-read.

Chris *"C-Mo"* Mason
San Angelo St. Basketball Hall Of Fame

Introduction

When I wrote **COACH "The Mediator Of Dreams And Destroyer Of Generations**, I had no idea the impact it would have on so many individuals present at the time or the impact at it would have on my present.

The internal freedom I experienced writing COACH along with the blessing of meeting and conversing with so many wonderful people, provided me with gratification I hadn't felt since high school basketball.

I got a chance to talk with others who were struggling mentally or had been struggling for years just like I was and had been.

COACH is my story and will always be the foundation and centerpiece for conversations I have pertaining to trauma and mental health.

I WAS ONLY FOUR-YEARS OLD "The Psyche Of A Broken Sole" is my "why."

My "why" to those who wanted to know why I was so angry, hurt, and still carried so much animosity in my heart.

FOUR-YEARS OLD is my "why" to why people dream and fight so hard for those dreams to come to fruition.

FOUR-YEARS OLD is my "why" to why my story *COACH* means so much to me.

My "why" to why the physical and mental struggles aren't barriers preventing progress, but motivation to achieve greatness.

IN MY THOUGHTS "The Evolution Of A Scarred Mind" is my "revelation."

Parlayed with *COACH* and *FOUR-YEARS OLD, SCARRED*

MIND IS my attempt to help people understand the importance of the people in their lives who have a major impact on their everyday existence, decision-making, and happiness.

Along with the people who allow them to have the same impact on their lives.

THE EVOLUTION OF A SCARRED MIND is a revolutionary battle of our thoughts fighting for the opportunity to heal from the past through understanding and acceptance.

A battle for freedom and a pathway to move forward and create new more memorable and meaningful thoughts.
THE EVOLUTION OF A SCARRED MIND provides us with the beauty of seeing our scars as beauty marks instead of ugly reminders.

More importantly, our evolution allows us to evolve and morph into the best version of our intellectual intelligence.

To have all the trauma and hardships manifest happiness and possible greatness while providing hope for mental stability and mental healing.

I hope my revelation, *IN MY THOUGHTS "The Evolution Of A Scarred Mind"* and my quotes resonate with the readers and allow them openings to find their pathway to happiness through their thoughts.

Jerry Alan Mason

Life Defining

4-14 Years Old
Growing Up Early

I start with four years old because of a memorable conversation that referenced me back to that age. Four years old also referenced me back to the beginning of my relationship with pain.

Those years, 4-14, are growing years. Experimenting and fun years. This evolution was the worst physically and mentally I think life has been for me.

Mainly because I was so young, in severe pain, and afraid. I wasn't mentally developed enough to understand "why me."

I had to grow up early without knowing how or what it meant to grow up.

After I fractured my foot while in the seventh grade, I truly believed I deserved all the bad things that had happened and were happening to me.

I felt I had to have done something wrong to deserve such pain and traumatic events at such a young age.

Before Jr. high, I loved playing baseball, football, and basketball. The pain would usually attack my body at night when I laid down.

Once I fractured my foot, that pain created an entirely different human within me.
The embarrassment, pain, adjustments, and depression will most likely dictate my thoughts and the results of that, for the rest of my life.

Because sports were such a part of the culture of Lamesa as they are in most states and countries, I couldn't imagine that culture not being a part of my every day.

So, I had to form a relationship with the pain knowing we both required a place in my soul.

My Jr. High years of playing the sports I loved were the worst.

As I progress through life, I get the question, "When are you going to settle down and commit to a relationship." My response would most times be, "I am settled down. It just happens to be with a life-defining relationship with pain, fear, and trauma."

Bobo

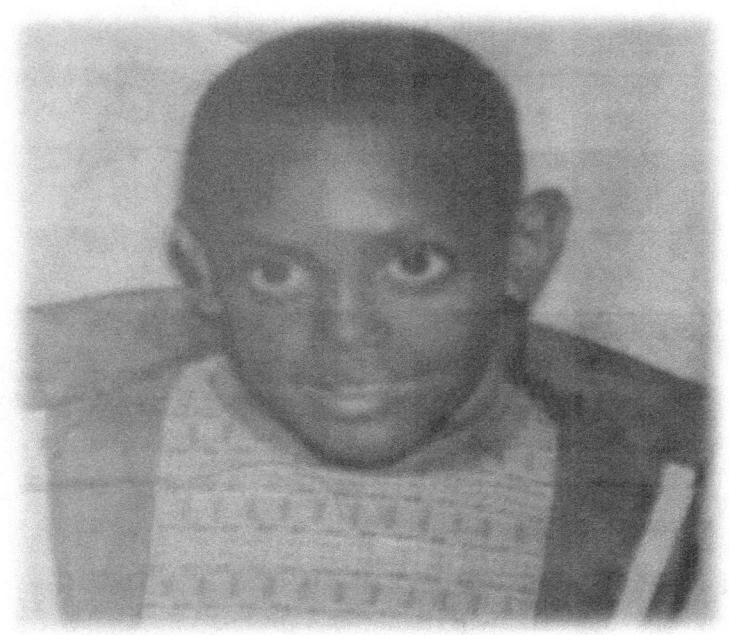

Evolution I
"Bobo"

Her Thoughts

Bo is fierce. Once our parents put a basketball goal outside our house, he would be out there all night playing by himself. All we could hear was the ball bouncing as he worked diligently to become the athlete he became. He also jumped rope for hours each morning and night.

Bo was dedicated and committed so his work didn't stop when everyone else did. His work ethic was tireless, and that extra work increased his endurance and made him the best possible version of himself.

I remember my brothers blasting onto the basketball scene together. As they both excelled, the craze for Lamesa basketball grew. The crowds would be packed outside hours before the game started. Just for an opportunity to get into an always jam-packed gym to watch Lamesa play. Every game no matter where they played was standing-room only.

The bigger the crowd, the better the show. They were never disappointed. My brother and his teammates not only became local but also regional and state celebrities. They all had different personalities and swag. People came from all over to watch them play.

The crowd would love to see Bo shoot from half-court at any time of the game. His mind was wild. They also loved to see him block shots and best of all, watch his variety of creative dunks. There was no three-point line in high school when he played. But most of his shots were from that distance or much further back. He rarely missed no matter where he shot from.

The minute he would let it fly from God knows where, the crowd would start yelling and screaming, "Money." If he got a steal or pass on the fast break from one of his teammates, most of the time it was a spectacular dunk. But you never knew with Bo. Everyone would be standing waiting and wanting a dunk, and he would pull up and shoot from deep with no one guarding him or stopping him from dunking. He was always in beast mode.

When he jumped to block a shot or get a rebound, it was like he was floating in the air.

While doing so, people in the crowd would say with awe, ***"Look at him fly."***

Bo didn't receive private lessons to get him better. He created his workouts and equipment. Before we got the basketball goal outside, they shot baskets in an orange oil can with a rubber ball. He made jump ropes out of extension cords until he somehow got a real jump rope.

He ran bleachers in the heat of the day at the football stadium. When they played basketball, they played outside in that scorching West Texas heat.

Not once did I hear Bo, Chris, or his teammates complain about the weather conditions. They were determined to be great. I had no idea Bo was dealing with the injuries and deficiencies he had. I learned like most people reading his books COACH and FOUR YEARS OLD.

It broke my heart for him as a sister. But it also made sense to me why he worked so hard. I am super proud to call him my brother and I love him with all my heart.

Monique Mason

Conversation From Within

Frozen in a glaze while feeling trapped in a maze, not knowing if my nights were nights or my days were days.

Trembling from the pain and always scared death was near,

Struggling so badly mentally that I could never think clearly.

Using sleep as an ally to protect me from my reality, afraid everyone around me could see and sense the fragility of my mentality.

Searching for someone who could empathize with my pain, is enough to drive any four-year-old kid insane.

Demons fighting deep inside my body, causing turmoil in my soul,

Fearing the morning sun creeping through the curtains, meaning pressure on my sole, causing havoc within me, this boy of thirteen, causing me to feel broken and old.

Decisions, decisions, I think to myself. Disillusioned as I contemplate which pair of shoes should I wear, I hear a voice, "good morning young fella," he says to me. "You only have one pair."

"Go away poverty, why are you here, why are you everywhere?"

Bobo

Relief

"When I would wake up in the morning as a kid while feeling the pain rush through me like a Tsunami, at that point I would feel normal and ok."

Bobo

Pain

"Sometimes it's worth the pain to avoid the irritation."

Bobo

Envision

"Sometimes, you have to envision the worst to make your reality consolation."

Bobo

Confused

"Sometimes as a kid, it's hard to decipher the difference between tough love and neglect."

Bobo

Understanding

"Cry because of your understanding when you want to feel better."

Bobo

Trauma

"If you give up on me because of your fears and I give up on me because it's my safe place, we have no chance at happiness."

Bobo

Demons

"It's sometimes easier to choose your fears and demons than trusting the process and its end result."

Bobo

Destiny

"Possibly, the crooked end of the stick points you to the straight path you need to reach your desired destination."

Bobo

Pillow

"As a kid when the pain got too unbearable for me at night, it always made me feel better to flip the pillow over."

Bobo

Succeed

"When all else fails, succeed. Contempt, consolation, and complacency are not an option."

Bobo

Tradition

"Tradition is a contagious monster. Without it, it's like trying to resuscitate a manikin. With it, tradition provides a pulse to the dream, hope for the dream, and a possibility that the dream could come true."

Bobo

Stubborn

"If you know something is bad or wrong and still let it mold into cement, it's virtually impossible to penetrate or fix."

Bobo

Let's Go

15-18 Years Old
High School Days

I prayed for jr. high to be over.
It couldn't have ended fast enough for me.
I had figured out how to navigate my back pain from four years old
to seventh grade. Trying to balance the back and foot pain during
jr. high was the WORST mental battle ever.

But once I got into high school, it had been two years of
strategizing, deceit, and contemplation.

After seeing the dr. and deciding surgery to repair my foot wasn't
best for me, I immediately created a persona and mindset that
would give me a chance to move forward.

Unsure of how to do so, but determined, at fifteen years old, I was
like, "Let's Go!"

So, the evolution of *Jerry "Bobo" Mason* began.
The pain and work became my friend. My way to mental stability
and stardom. It all paid off.

During this evolution, I was able to feel like I was important. Not
in the eyes, minds, and hearts of people, but important to myself.

This was my most rewarding and fun evolution. I got a chance to
feel and experience how I wanted the rest of my life to be.

Jerry *"Bobo"* Mason

Evolution II
Jerry "Bobo" Mason
"JBM"

Cedric In His Thoughts

Even though we grew up with challenges and struggles like a lot of families, I remember my childhood being fun. Fun because of my siblings, Chris, Bobo, and Monique. We argued, fought, and competed against each other every day. We played a lot of games, always competing in pairs. Chris and Monique versus me and Bo. Those were always the teams, no matter what game, race, or whatever we played.

We used to have classic battles which sometimes led to arguments and fights. I think that's how we learned to compete and found our desire to win. More than anything, to hate losing. As the youngest of four, I grew up idealizing my siblings as we progressed through our childhood via sports. The constant talk I would hear about me not having a chance to be as good as my brothers motivated me.

Not in a jealous way. I loved and respected how good my brothers had gotten at all sports. It motivated me to want to be good as well. Maybe even better. Once they got into high school, Chris and Bo were all-star and all-state selections in basketball and Monique was the same in volleyball. Not even the chatter I would hear was needed to motivate me to want to achieve the same feats. It was in me, and I wanted to achieve and worked to achieve the same accolades. It was part of the competitive, winning, wanting to be the best attitude we all possessed.

However, the comparisons and criticism did sometimes hurt me. But I used it as an ally instead of a crutch to propel me forward. Starting on the varsity basketball team with Bo, my sophomore year was the toughest, most taxing, and most humbling experience I'd ever experienced. Bo was obsessed with winning and being the best. His obsession caused him to be irritable, demanding, mean, and selfish and the best leader and role model we could have had.

I remember him being mad at me during a game and shouting at me, "Come on bro, quit being weak. You're no Mason." That hurt me, but it was his way of pushing me and protecting me at the same time. He was a different beast. I had no idea he was going through his physical issues. As we got older and I learned his motivation, need, and passion for success, I respected him even more and was grateful he pushed me the way he did.

I love and appreciate my siblings for being great role models for me. I appreciate them pushing and molding me into the player I became and the man I am.

Cedric *"C-Lo"* Mason

Things

Some things mean more to us than others ever will, because no one should tell us what we want or how we need to feel.

Some things will never be the way we think they should be because if they were there would be no challenge and life would be too good.

Some things will never change. They will keep chingling like sounds from chimes; so, therefore, I try to express to you my up and down times.

Some things will sting a little and some will cut like a knife, and I try to patch the pieces and write for you… my life.

Jerry *"Bobo"* Mason

Compromise

"Pain is a powerful asset when navigated with the respect and understanding of its potential."

Jerry *"Bobo"* Mason

Engulfed

"I didn't go to bed or wake up needing a drink. I never longed for cigarettes or nicotine. Nor did I desire to smoke marijuana, cocaine, or heroin. I went to bed and woke up needing basketball. I craved the affect basketball had on my every day, and I longed for the affect basketball had on my soul. I needed the way this sport made me feel, and how it gave me chills. I desired and was addicted to an orange rock."

Jerry *"Bobo"* Mason

Competition

"The addictiveness to success is dangerous."

Jerry *"Bobo"* Mason

Rise

"Sometimes the most gratifying rise to the top comes from someone who started from an ugly bottom."

Jerry *"Bobo"* Mason

Dependable

"I get high on knowing that every day someone's happiness depends on my greatness."

Jerry *"Bobo"* Mason

Teammates

"Do what you have to do to make sure your teammates don't lose until they can be the reason your team wins."

Jerry *"Bobo"* Mason

Deficiencies

"To be a great leader and desire the best results for your teams' success, you can't only work for you. You must put in extra work to accommodate for the deficiencies each teammate has."

Jerry *"Bobo"* Mason

Bitter Pill

"To know someone is better than you because you allow them to be, should be a bitter pill to swallow."

Jerry *"Bobo"* Mason

Prepared

"Even though God has the final decision in our outcome, with the abilities blessed to you, work your hardest for your outcome to be successful."

Jerry *"Bobo"* Mason

Difference Maker

"It's necessary to fit it when it's mandatory, but real winners know when it's time to rise above adversity when things need to get done."

Jerry *"Bobo"* Mason

Star

"It's impossible to be a star when you only dream as high as the clouds."

Jerry *"Bobo"* Mason

Accountable

"Being disgusted or angry with myself during a moment, motivated me to be better for future moments."

Jerry *"Bobo"* Mason

Denial

"It's a gambling problem whether its dice or sports or you win or lose. The common denominator is the addiction."

Jerry *"Bobo"* Mason

Leaders

"Leaders don't win and want fame nor lose and not take the blame."

Jerry *"Bobo"* **Mason**

Proactive

"In order to achieve the success and dreams you desire, you have to be proactive in your want."

Jerry *"Bobo"* Mason

Fragile

"Being mad is carrying anger. Being hurt means someone you loved betrayed your trust."

Jerry *"Bobo"* Mason

Voices

"The silence of success is deafening."

Jerry *"Bobo"* Mason

Mean

"Mean is not a look, it's an attitude."

Jerry *"Bobo"* Mason

The Gamble

You must work at it to have a chance. You have to work extra hard to be great. You must be willing to lose it all, to be great."

Jerry *"Bobo"* Mason

Legend

"To become a legend in the mind, heart, and souls of your peers and community should be a dream of every athlete. To create an atmosphere neither you nor they can ever forget. To etch a picture money can't buy but will be tattooed in their memories forever."

Jerry *"Bobo"* Mason

Country Boy

"I could not grasp nor comprehend the honor and magnitude of being chosen as a 1st Team High School basketball All-American. I didn't even know how big Texas was. I just knew cotton, dust, and tumbleweeds."

Jerry *"Bobo"* Mason

Resuscitation
18-31 Years Old
Fantasy To Reality

This evolution was a very humbling, hurtful, embarrassing, stressful, confusing, and challenging time for me.

I didn't achieve my goal and dream of being drafted into the NBA. I was very disappointed in two men who I felt contributed to the derailment of my progress and progression. I felt like they were selfish dream killers.

I was in a horrible state. I was embarrassed and felt like a failure. I felt hurt and betrayed but only blamed myself. I had my first son, Jeremy, during Evolution II and my second son, Jordan, during Evolution III. So, my priorities and responsibilities had to change.

I had to find a new profession even though I continued to be heartbroken by the same dream. This evolution was the beginning of a new era in my life. Besides my boys, I found something that could resuscitate my soul.

Chase

A-Train, Chase, Big Woo-My 7' roommates and brothers.

Evolution III
"Chase"

"Trouble In His Thoughts"

When I think of Jerry Mason, many things come to my mind. Not only was he my college teammate at Texas Tech University, but he's also my brother. Mason is a very kind person. A pure soul. He would give his last dollar to a stranger on the street.

As far as basketball goes, in my eyes, nobody played it better. I met Chase during a couple of high school all-star games. I was immediately blown away by his talent. He could jump out of the gym. He played much bigger than 6'3 and he was also the best and most pure shooter I'd ever seen.

As that summer progressed and I learned Chase had committed to Texas Tech, the idea of playing with him intrigued me. Therefore, I then committed to playing college basketball at Texas Tech University. I didn't learn until many years later about his pain, brokenness, and hardships.

Like most people, even his family members, I learned about his struggles during his youth from reading the two books that he wrote.

Once again, I was blown away by him. To learn he had been through so much as a kid broke my heart for my brother.

I remember him always asking me to help him up while we were in college after he had been sitting for a while or we were about to go somewhere. I thought nothing of it as we all were hurting or sore from the rigorous workouts and long days.

He never complained about his severe pain at that time or ever. He'd just politely ask me, *"Trouble, help me up please bro."* As I learned and reflected more, I once again was fascinated by Chase. I was fascinated by what he had achieved despite the injuries he had been dealing with.

I knew what it took to become a Division I (D-I) athlete and basketball player. That he could achieve that along with all the accolades and accomplishments is virtually impossible for any human to do. It's still hard for me to comprehend. If I could describe Chase in one word, it would be "Professional." He was an NBA talent. I believe he would have been a star in the NBA.

During practices or pre-game warm-up, Chase would do post moves with the centers then run to the other end and do guard work with the guards. His versatility, creativity, athletic ability, and shooting were something different than I and most had ever seen.

I could go on forever about my brother Chase But I will finish by saying thank you to him for all his support through my good and tough times. He always puts people's pain and well-being before his own. I want to congratulate him on his years of perseverance and his success as a Coach and an Author.

James "Double J" Johnson

Prayer

As the tears flowed softly down my face, I closed my eyes to pray, thanking God for my past and hopefully another day.

But as I prayed, I began to get selfish and lose my train of thought, and began to explain to God the tears and why I felt so distraught.

"You see God, I'm so hurt and confused, and I really can't understand," "Why did you allow him to do me this way, why did you make him the man?"

"You're the only God there is, but yet he had all the power," "He took my ally and turned her into my enemy, which turned my sweet dreams sour."

"You can't do this Jerry and you can't do that Jerry, is all I could hear him saying," So, I closed my eyes tighter and tighter as I continued crying and praying.

"Why God why, does it have to be me, in a position that's so unbearable," I knew he wasn't going to answer me and there was no answer to this parable.

While crying and praying, I regained my train of thought, knowing I was only fooling myself and it wasn't God's fault.

That choice I made because of love now haunted me all day and night, I knew I had lost my love in the battle, but I just couldn't lose my fight.

"Please God, please help me breathe. He's invaded my soul and taken my oxygen away," "Please God I beg of you sir, please don't let him do me this way."

So, I finished thanking for today and praying for peace tomorrow, Crying and hoping the tears would stop flowing or I just drown in my sorrow.

"Thank you, God. Thank you for blessing me with the opportunity to shine," "Thank you for allowing me to have a love I can be in love with, as she is so divine."

Amen was the thing I said before I opened my eyes to the dark, Still feel the pain deep in my soul, because my love had left her mark.

Chase

Naive

"It's imperative to be cognizant if you're the prize or the pawn of the game. The disillusionment and the lack of knowing can cause irreversible damage to any chance at trust and/or happiness."

Chase

Constitution

"A person's trials and tribulations are their constitution. It's hard to change or make amendments to that which is etched in stone."

Chase

Racism

"A racist mind is equivalent to an unfulfilled and uneducated ego."

Chase

Irrelevant

"How do you make yourself irrelevant in someone else's journey when you're the most important element for their journey to be a success?"

Chase

Perspective

"Sometimes the dark is the only way or place that trauma will allow a person to see the little light they possess within them."

Chase

Two-Sided Coin

"You earn failure just as much as you earn success."

Chase

Triggers

"Other people's choices don't dictate whether you are good enough or not. They are just other people's choices that trigger your choices."

Chase

No Pain

"They say, "no pain, no gain." But who must endure the pain, what is it and what are they trying to gain?"

Chase

Recruiter

"Why lead a thirsty horse to water when you know the water is contaminated?"

Chase

Hater

"There's a big difference between a "has been" and a "wannabe." Although a "has been," is has, he was. Even though a "wannabe," wants to be, he never will.

Chase

Obstacles

"To not endure the obstacles of the present but continue to carry negative results from the past, leads to a beautiful blossoming future one will never experience."

Chase

Reality

"Reality is a humbling creature."

Chase

Impact

"It's harder to have an impact with winners in convincing them to trust and change than it is with losers."

Chase

Lurking

"Possible success lies dormant waiting to explode within the freedom and opportunity provided."

Chase

Zombies

"Dreamers without the encouragement, optimism, and freedom to dream are walking zombies accepting their fate."

Chase

Defeated

"It's hard to formulate new dreams when the old ones didn't manifest."

Chase

Liar

"Why come get me if you don't want me?"

Chase

Brotherhood

"Besides my own physical and mental trauma, being a college athlete is a beast of its own. There's beauty within the lights and demons during the nights but the friendships and brotherhood you build with your teammates is better than any therapist money can buy."

Chase

Queens, Double J, 2A, Chase, DB

DB, 2A, Double J, B Brown, Chase

Content
31-41 Years Old
New Challenges

I finally accepted my basketball career and my dreams were over. I had been coaching for about seven years at this point and although I never missed work or cheated on my profession, I wasn't fully invested in anything, not even being a coach.

Just my sorrows, trauma, and heartbreak, and basketball occupied my soul and emotions. Once I was content with my present and reality, I became committed to being the best coach, role model, and parent that I could be. It was me growing up and starting an entirely new life. I had no idea this evolution would be so challenging and rewarding. I had always felt like my understanding of my pain and how to navigate it at such a young age, allowed me to mature faster than most kids. That has benefited me throughout each evolution.

Even though I became content with my losses and failures, I gained so much more during this evolution. I was granted the blessing of assisting in raising Jordan when he came to live with me. I also became a head coach, which gave me a greater opportunity to be the mediator of many dreams. This evolution allowed me to see and spend more time with my brothers as we all shared the same profession. It also gave me the chance to meet so many new people and make family-like friends. It was the first time in my life I felt like I was coming out of my darkness and controlling my light.

Coach Mason

Evolution IV
"Coach Mason"

Unwavering Dream

In love with a love that doesn't soul me, in love with my fantasy
that will never be.

A figment of my imagination but captured mentally by your strict
plantation.

Grasping for air within the grips of your passion; wanting to shine
through the eyes of your fashion.

Hold me! Hold me! Hold me please, I beg of you omnipotent one,
as I fall to my knees.

The coldness of your ignoring me pulsates me into a shiver; I feel
the frosting in the failure of my liver.

Telling me, "Friend you have nothing else to give her," "she's not
going to bend for your wants, she won't even quiver."

Coach Mason

Seasons

"Once an athlete enters Jr. High school, there are only twenty-four seasons until their Saturday."

Coach Mason

Gratification

"The place that allows you to have the greatest impact may be the same place that provides you the least gratification."

Coach Mason

Meticulous

"Basketball is a game of sounds, numbers, and progressions."

Coach Mason

Sacrifice

"Sometimes you have to sacrifice important things to protect more important things."

Coach Mason

Feedback

"Help with helpful and optimistic feedback instead of pessimistic emotions tied to selfish expectations."

Coach Mason

Reverse Psychology

"It's possible to hold your kids accountable and love them at the same time. Accountability is love."

Coach Mason

Elevate

"Don't modify your dreams, elevate your grind."

Coach Mason

Winners

"You beat lesser opponents with fear. You beat better opponents with a fight."

Coach Mason

Asset

"If your biggest asset is your presence and you're never present, then your presence is no longer impactful or an asset."

Coach Mason

Mental Fortitude

"The conflict comes when you're strong physically and weak mentally or vice versa."

Coach Mason

Embrace

"Solid work. Embrace the beauty within the opportunity."

Coach Mason

Excuse

"Nothing good happens when you're looking for an excuse to make an excuse."

Coach Mason

Pessimist

"What have you done to help to deserve the right to complain?"

Coach Mason

Mediate

"Why mediate when the result of the mediation only benefits the mediator?"

Coach Mason

Enemy

"I'm not your enemy; life is your enemy... I am just the messenger."

Coach Mason

Trust

"Don't listen to be sensitive to my words, listen to feel my passion."

Coach Mason

Basketball

"Basketball is not a game, it's a business. It's a showcase of hard work becoming art. It's a representation of your mental creativity and physical persistence. Basketball is its entity, creating a space for individualism and freedom. Basketball is my life."

Coach Mason

Habits

"The habits that we allow our kids to create today are the same habits that will decide and dictate the culture of theirs and our future."

Coach Mason

Committed

"If you'll always stay one day, and one point ahead of your opponent, you'll never be behind and you'll never lose."

Coach Mason

Test

"If you break them early, you won't have to worry about them later. If you bend early despite their want and need for discipline, they will tear down and ruin any chance of structure and tradition you may want to build."

Coach Mason

Responsibility

"It's your responsibility as a parent and coach to raise, prepare, and teach your kids how to make you proud when it's time for them to perform. It's the performance that generates all the emotions and criticism."

Coach Mason

Praise

"Make sure your deficiencies come before, and your praise comes after the prepositional phrase."

Coach Mason

Winning

"Get a stop, get a rebound, and get a bucket… time after time."

Coach Mason

Structure

"You have no right to criticize, chastise, or discipline kids if you have no structure as a mentor, parent, teacher, or coach."

Coach Mason

Fighting Back

41 Years Old-Present
The Evolution of the Man

So many tragic things happened during this evolution. Enough to where I was offered clinical depression assistance. Jordan left for college. Which wasn't depressing at all but took me back to a lonely place I was at before he moved in with me.

I went through a probate situation I didn't ask to be a part of that was very invasive which never manifested. It was very idiotic of me to allow myself to get engulfed in someone else's toxic drama. It was the beginning and maybe the catalyst for all the ugliness I allowed to follow. I feel the probated situation derailed me from the progress I had made and the healing I felt in the previous evolutions. I also changed and lost that job, had two car repossessions, lost my house, and some people I thought loved or cared about me.

The most tragic of all, we lost our beautiful mother, who died in May of 2019. The probate situation was about a ten-year waste and the rest happened between a year and a half span of time. Parlayed with Covid. Thankfully in a sad way, I had been through so much as a kid, teenager, and adult, that the events that happened during this evolution had no chance of breaking me. Not one chance.

"Sometimes you have to expect the worst to make your reality consolation."

So, I fought back. I thought basketball was my only path to a chance at fulfillment and happiness. But God showed me otherwise. I became a published author, poet, writer, and ghostwriter and got an opportunity to be a head coach again. This is the complete evolution of the man that God created me to be up to this point and preparing me to be for the future.

Jerry Alan Mason

Evolution V
Jerry Alan Mason
"Jam"

Daily Grind

As I dream of the morning anticipating daydreaming of the night, seeing all the wrongs of my present, praying they soon become right.

The sunlight beaming on my desire not to excite my immobility, Igniting the dendrites that put pressure on my mentality.

"Should I go left, should I go right?" "Just stay Chase. Stay, stay!" "Dream Bo, dream." "Just pray Bo. Pray, pray!"

As the stars of the morning sun glow bright through the dark blinds, I formulate my path to survival, despite the tortures of my mind.

One step at a time Jerry, one careful move at a time. One dollar, one quarter, one nickel, one dime. Respecting the evolution of its control and power and its effect on my daily grind.

Jerry Alan Mason

Progressions

"Life is a series of progressions, and if we learn to master them it will provide us with the comfort, and consistency we need to survive in this chaotic world."

Jerry Alan Mason

Legacy

"Live your life as an adverb and let your epithet describe you in adjectives."

Jerry Alan Mason

Passion and Desire

"Passion allows you the ability to feel the embrace and absorb the storm. Desire tempts you to travel through the storm, no matter what."

Jerry Alan Mason

Torture

"Dealing with pain and trauma is a twenty-four hour a day job that doesn't pay very well."

Jerry Alan Mason

Victim of Circumstances

"Trauma hides in your soul waiting for the perfect time to surface and be primary in controlling every aspect of your life."

Jerry Alan Mason

Roller Coaster

"Life is a series of roller coaster rides. We just don't get to choose when or where we ride or how enjoyable we want the ride to be. It just happens in an adverb kind of way."

Jerry Alan Mason

Impatient

"Desire and greed without fear of consequences sometimes has people trying to wrangle their future without having the proper rope to capture their present."

Jerry Alan Mason

Motivation

"XXL is content. XL is a challenge and motivation to fight harder and do better."

Jerry Alan Mason

Embarrassing

"The biggest ego killer is dropping something in public that you need or want while knowing you can't bend and pick it up, with everyone looking at you."

Jerry Alan Mason

Enslavement

"To be free from slavery but enslave your mind with the personalities and perspectives of slavery still makes you a slave. No matter what race you are."

Jerry Alan Mason

Complicated

"Complication is a fear of choosing. Sometimes we make our complications as complicated as we need them to be so that we don't have to decide or choose."

Jerry Alan Mason

Oblivious

"Freedom is just a word most people use to not acknowledge how oblivious they are to the mindset and world they have enslaved themselves in. There's a boss to every action and a consequence for everything we do."

Jerry Alan Mason

Damaged

"Falling in love happens instantly. However, we dissect things to make ourselves feel comfortable in not pursuing the passion we feel. So, we slowly take our time mentally breaking it down, tearing it apart, and falling out of love."

Jerry Alan Mason

Reinforcement

"No one looks or is built better than me in my clothes because it's only me in my clothes."

Jerry Alan Mason

Sports and Love

"When you play the game, there's always a possibility you could lose."

Jerry Alan Mason

Fall

"We fall in love with someone who internalizes our pain. We fall in lust with someone who fulfills our desires."

Jerry Alan Mason

Content

"I can be your friend and still not trust you as a person."

Jerry Alan Mason

Fake

"I don't want from you the things that suit me. I want from you
the best you can genuinely give me."

Jerry Alan Mason

Ashamed

"Some people crawl from room to room even though they have the capability to walk. They do so because they are ashamed of their reality and shortcomings with the fear of looking at their reflection in the mirror which lurks between the two rooms."

Jerry Alan Mason

Create

"Create your wonderful masterpiece from all the painful, trying, fearful, hurtful, embarrassing moments and events that you've encountered in your past to make a beautiful productive present and future."

Jerry Alan Mason

Certified vs Qualified

"Certified fills the void for the non-certified. Qualified fills the void for the blessing, and fills the cracks in the holes of the dreams and dreamers and let's God's plan do the rest."

Jerry Alan Mason

Corpse

"Any person functioning every day without hope or a dream is equivalent to a corpse with no life flowing through their body."

Jerry Alan Mason

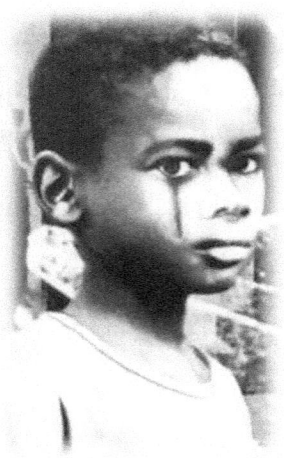

Matthew,

Our evolution has guided us to this point, my friend. You couldn't have made it without me; I couldn't have lived without you living inside me.

So many nights we made my brothers think, feel compassion, and laugh as you and I cried to sleep after our performance was done. So many sad lonely days I talked to you, with you, as you listened closely and patiently without judgment. The logic and depth of your delicate responses to my cry for help and understanding of my pain were lifesaving.

The quotes your mind helped me formulate laid dormant inside my soul my entire life. Selfishly, I used them to benefit and soothe me only. Now I share your wisdom, our pain, and our metamorphosis with the world. It's our evolution from the dark, scarred, and scary past to a bright and attainable future. I had to keep you alive to keep me from contemplating on dying, you saved me!

So many things have happened since we created each other, things that were hurtful, painful, traumatic, fun, joyous and unimaginable. *LIFE!* Our life together has happened since we first met Matthew.

Because no one could physically see you and only I knew you existed, I have been the beneficiary of all the good things and the recipient of all the bad.

But you, Matthew, are the reason I shined and the strength that guided and helped me persevere through all the pain, tears, trauma, fears, cold lonely nights, and hot pretentious days.

I thank God for you.
I am you. You are me.
Because of you, I BLOSSOM!
I LOVE YOU.

Bobo

I Blossom

I Blossom through the wintery ice,
I Blossom even when my dreams aren't nice.

I Blossom because I have no choice,
I Blossom through my pessimistic voice.

I Blossom although my sun never shines.
I Blossom even when my pain overwhelms and controls my mind.

I Blossom through my ups and downs,
I Blossom through my internal explosive sounds.

I've Blossomed through my depression over the years,
I continue to Blossom through all my failures and all my fears.

I Blossom because my tears continue to water my present.

Jerry Alan Mason

About The Author

Jerry "Bobo" Mason was born and raised in Lamesa Texas. He's the 2nd born son of four children to Jerry and Velma Mason. As a young kid, Jerry fell in love with sports and winning. Lamesa was a town filled with talent, pride, and tradition. Sports was the mediator that bonded friends, families, and a community together. This atmosphere was an addiction Jerry "Bobo" Mason couldn't kick. He was hooked on baseball, football, and basketball at a very young age.

The author exposes his true-life story starting from the age of four. He reveals to his audience, while at four, suffering from severe back pain. Through that pain and agony as a child, the thought of not being able to play sports kept Jerry going.

Trauma struck Jerry again as a thirteen-year-old. This tragedy coupled with the pain he had been experiencing in his back, would cause Jerry physical, mental, and emotional damage that would alter the rest of his decision-making and life; because of his passion for sports, mainly basketball, Jerry decided to move forward with both traumatic injuries in hopes of achieving his dreams.

Jerry received great recognition and numerous awards during his high school career. Including becoming a first-team All-American. All despite his physical and mental challenges.

The author parlayed his struggles and success into a basketball scholarship at Texas Tech University. There, he would accomplish great feats but face adversity that would alter the course of his life. That collegiate journey led Jerry to write and publish his first novel, **COACH "The Mediator of Dreams and Destroyer of Generations."**

This novel would become an instant tool in helping the mediators of sports and life journeys understand the dynamic impact they can have on the ones they are mediating in life.

After chasing a long-time childhood dream to play NBA basketball, Jerry became a successful award-winning coach. Through his coaching journey, Jerry was able to fulfill some childhood dreams but more importantly, coaching allowed Jerry to begin to heal mentally and emotionally.

Teaching and helping students and athletes became a tremendous passion for him and prompted him to write his 2nd non-fiction novel, **I Was Only Four Years Old "The Psyche of a Broken Sole."** This novel deals with today's issues of the prominent presence of mental health issues.

This novel collaborates with the message from his first novel, "COACH." Both novels were written by Author Jerry Mason as a guide to help the world know the many factors that can contribute to the mental health pandemic. The author bares his soul in each novel to allow everyone to engulf his journey in hopes of helping the world respect the fragility of each human's mind.

Author
Jerry "Bobo" Mason